LEARNING BEYOND COVID

DR DHEERAJ MEHROTRA DR USHAVATI SHETTY

Contents

Preface

Learning Beyond COVID is a capsule towards making learning a priority with the VUCA world in progress. The Volatile, Uncertain, Complex and Ambiguous spectrum is all set to devise and explore new challenges with the march of time and tide. The book presents some evaluated facts and information that bend the post- Pandemic views and make us ready to confront the uncertain times ahead.

Covid or no Covid, learning has to be a priority.

Cheers & Happy Reading.

Authors!

CHAPTER ONE

The Priority

LEARNING BEYOND COVID

Paperless Classrooms !!! The post-pandemic period allows us to reimagine what schools and schooling are for and advocate for a re-schooled society in which our investment in schools builds and develops community.

Today's learners are digital natives. They are accustomed to getting information and meeting their needs with a click of a button in a user-friendly, personal and customisable way. Students want their learning experience to meet their interests, time constraints and academic needs.

Tech-savvy- Learners are even more technologically savvy, demanding, confident and focused. Contrary to the old-school traditions in English, math, social studies and science, we'll need to redesign curriculum and courses to reflect the skills that are mandated by emerging economies and technologies. Skills such as coding, design, sustainability and financial literacy will have to be integrated and taught in the classroom.

Real-life experience- Schools will have to offer more ways for students to gain real-world experience that applies to their future careers. Schools should provide opportunities for students and include internship programs in companies. Rather than limiting students inside a classroom, schools can create more opportunities for students to gain valuable technical skills through real-world application.

Breaking the norm - The world has already witnessed that the concept of 9-5 jobs in the office is also decreasing as people get an enormous scope for earning by sitting at their home and working online. As the world has witnessed many technological changes, many things have changed since then. An email has replaced letters, and WhatsApp and Facebook have almost substituted human interaction.

New methods- Blended learning, flipped classrooms and BYOD (Bring Your Device) for education—personalised learning at one's own pace and speed.

Mentor - The teacher would now be the mentor, clarifier and problem-solving specialist. Examination patterns will change entirely with the increased use of online quizzes, group projects, and group discussions.

Global inclusive learning - It's not very far when we will see students from all over the world attending the same classes and interacting with each other. No one will have to miss out on an education, and students are much more likely to enjoy learning.

CHAPTER TWO

THE EDUDEMIC

Post-COVID- An End to Online Befooling! The Edudemic.

The alarming spectrum delivers the learning to the aspect of teaching online for schools has been in action over a couple of years. For sure, the third wave proved the dis-interest attributes in action. The schools are sorry to involve the students and the parents with promises to keep but not in motion. The online spectrum is a failed projection and has been proved majorly. Alarming. We call the call. No education. No Schooling? But a fancy TECH Candy integration. Sorry to say!

Well, the priority is low to spectrum. The teachers find the classrooms empty. The children are away from connecting. The learning is diminishing to zero! What are we up

to? Surprisingly the defined approach towards learning is taken a back seat to the segment which relates to once a priority. The activation desires the ready reckoner to manage education by the concerned, including the Government. In India, we aim at approaching comfort and safety with the closure of schools. The segment contains the outcome of many other excuses that relate to elections or more. For sure, the scientific evidence for schools as COVID-19 hotspots is fragile. A study in Spain looked at data from over 1 million children of all ages in schools and found that the R-Value (Rate of Virus Spread) is well less than one for all school students. The R-value is lower for lower ages and as standard as 0.2 for pre-primary children; hence the practice of closing schools appears unscientific.

How do I, as an educator, manage that? Can online learning be the ultimate solution to tasks? Not so, surprisingly so. Teachers and the parents need to gel together to prioritise learning with the conjunction towards learning as a prime approach rather than grasp the notion of closure of schools with the spectrum towards safety. Bells are ringing in countries where we have a heavy load of cases.

But for sure, taking a measure like this is like closing the chapters of learning for the future workforce for some time. This may lead to a bleak future for the nation in particular. I stand firm to undertaking as a priority.

My personal experience as a head of school highlights a novel spectrum to route this significance for the cause of quality education. The ratio is bleak towards the unaware specified interest of the students via the online or offline learning segment. The educators need a preface to the exact detail and relate at large numbers via brainstorming to narrate the strategies to follow up in directive for a better cause.

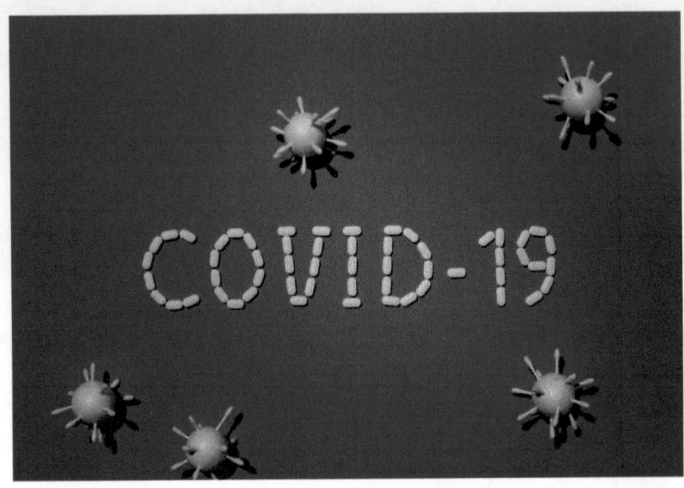

The system needs to be re-framed on how best to deliver the knowledge of the new age and the attention to live with corona as a striker for the new page for living and learning periodically.

The concern remains unanswered. Is it a pandemic scarier or the Edudemic? The bridge that has been constructed between online and remote learning has to take a page with the march of time. We just cannot and better never forget the standard portals for the classrooms and their importance.

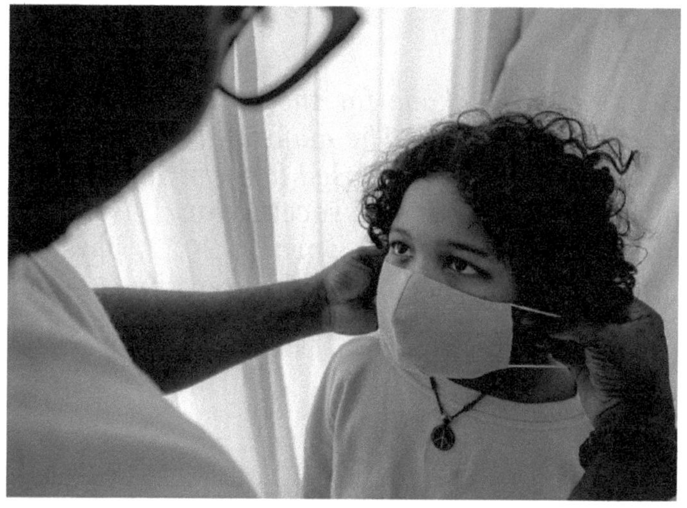

This bridge of learning gap that COVID has widened has also resulted in the investment in the infrastructure to a large extent. The purpose also dwells on the move on the additional emphasis on well-being and reskilling being promoted by the boards specifically. No doubt in terms of boosting the long-term growth but counts on the importance of re-opening the schools on priority.

Quoting one of the write ups' by Janmejaya Sinha, Chairman, BCG India, "With due respect to school education, the situation is dire. Data shows that more than 70% of the students have not received any significant educational input online.

A one-time package for the safe reopening of schools is required. The majority of India's one million schools have closed for two years. Some have been used as vaccination/ isolation centres. As we look to open in 2022, physical infrastructure needs to be revamped, and provisions for forward-looking health and safety measures.

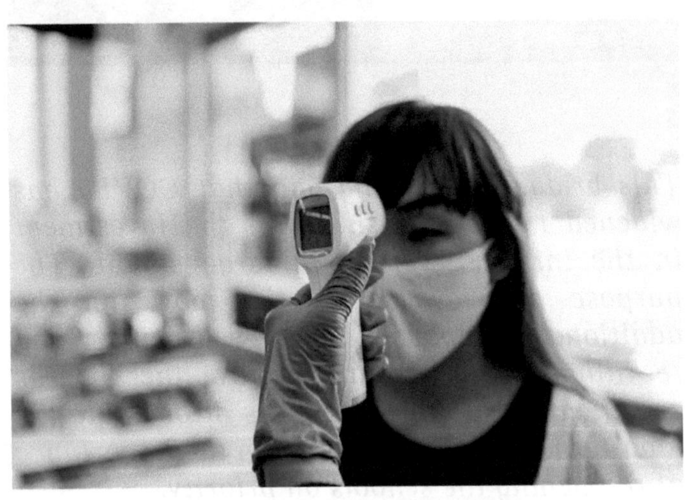

We as educators reflect a measure on the devastating impact of school closure, as by closing schools for this extended and providing just online education; we have violated

children's rights in a big way unconsciously. Even the unreasonable response to Omicron has had an impact, especially on children. Unfortunately, the schools have become an easy and soft target for politicians; closing the schools provides them with the benefit of being seen as "doing something" to being "Caring and Concerned" to containing COVID 19.

The concern lies in fact measuring, may it for the reality of the online learning, with no experiential learning, with no interaction in a real sense, the question remains unanswered with a concern, Does online education constitute education? I wonder and worry both. It is for sure a poor replacement for physical classes. The children, mainly in the pre-primary and the primary, can learn and be socially and emotionally involved. Quoting the survey report, from Sept. 2021, students' reading and writing levels have declined, with nearly half of them unable to read more than a few rods. More than a third of them were not studying at all.

We, the educator, reflect on the learning with a preface of Priority Learning first among ourselves as the students use their home classrooms, substituting their living rooms as learning platforms professionally. This has come by storm to page their comfort and capsuled their intelligence to a limit only with no physical connection and disruptions like that of actual classrooms. This makes their yesterdays as today and tomorrow with a stereotype living spectrum, targeting their limited learning and limited knowledge as a preface.

The answer lies in our heads, not the search via the laptops.

CHAPTER THREE

Teaching Tool Kit Post COVID

I was teaching in unprecedented times!

Out of nowhere, I went over this word VUCA, Volatile, Uncertain, Complex, and Ambiguous, distinguishing the new world request of range with no decision except for an approach to confronting the difficulties changing over them into favourable circumstances.

Without a doubt, the world is confronting a difficult time today. Nobody was at any point arranged for this and will at any moment be. The need we the people must have a deduction today towards having a bunch of essential abilities, information and demeanour, and business purchases these at a cost.

Understanding the VUCA World, the better! The abbreviation VUCA - Volatile, Uncertain, Complex, and Ambiguous - was authored during the 1990s. It depicts numerous individuals‘ experiences of their work environment incredibly well.

In this sort of climate, it tends to be challenging to feel like you are adapting - not to mention flourishing. The abbreviation VUCA -

Volatile, Uncertain, Complex, and Ambiguous - was instituted during the 1990s. It depicts numerous individuals' experiences of their work environment amazingly well. In the learning environment, the learners, particularly the students, need to come back to a supportive, friendly atmosphere, where their learning loss and socio-emotional needs are recognised, dwelled, curated as per the new world order acknowledged by the educators at large. These notions and craftings are required to help them get back on track. Let us revisit the fact that one of the key lessons learnt throughout the crisis is the importance of engaging parents and communities in pupils' learning process. And this must continue!

In this sort of climate, it may be not easy to feel like you are adapting - not to mention flourishing. Driving in a VUCA World - Leadership in the hours of Crisis is the new world order. We truly are seeing a remarkable change on the planet, and no part of our life

is immaculate by this change. From the unexpected change in our way of life to the tremendous shift in mentality, the present circumstance has constrained us all to think fast, think extraordinary, and raise versatility. Professional life is the same. In the genuine sense, the world right currently exemplifies the VUCA reasoning; Volatile, Uncertain, Complex, and Ambiguous. We were not ready for this unexpected development, and many are confused about how to adapt to this and push forward. Convenient solutions will presently don't work; this change is somewhat perpetual.

It implies that we should rethink and re-adjust every technique for activity, thinking, acting, and being. Going ahead, mental and enthusiastic well-being balance has gotten basic on an ongoing premise. The capacity to re-adjust ranges of abilities, practices, and activities according to the progressions on the planet is a consuming worry for us all.

We are affected by this in some structure or the other. What is required is Mental Health, Resilience, Self consideration and inclusivity. On the off chance that organisations are unequipped for sympathy, we can venture up and connect with companions and family members in trouble.

The Covid times require that extra portion of local area administration and social awareness for sure companions. We can start little—every single one of us. Keeping yourself propelled in any event, during the current situation where torment enduring passing lockdown dejection world has halted. Inspiration comes from the inside equilibrium of the brain, body soul. In this infuriating situation, keep a quiet, adjusted, formed outlook keeping yourself propelled, self-inspired and forcing others as the new practice. "Keeping yourself roused in any event, during the current situation". Much as we like to consider these as reasonable and impartial and fearlessly take cutbacks in our step, the playing. At the point when an acquiring part loses his employment, the family's funds are seriously affected.

This is undoubtedly Sad and lamentable. The vulnerability is troubling. A few families think it's extreme to try and meet routine costs—some need to plunge into their resources. As far as strength and holding power, the family and the business are extraordinary.

The individuals who have lost their positions are, in this way, taking a gander at a significant stretch of joblessness, cooped up for the most part inside their homes. Many would have managed their circumstance in protection without upsetting the family. What would we be able to do is comes a priority for all at this hour as educators, too on priority. Start Small, Start some online business. Investigate some revenue of yours as a calling. Check the old recollections to be content.

Have a go at cutting your costs and requests. Be together. Efficient attempt alternatives. You were searching for various acquiring choices, regardless of their less; however, the great. Beware of conveying on the web range of instructing/preparing/directing/the majority worldwide.

That is absolutely how I felt! As an educator. The teaching is on with no real students, in real-time physical classrooms. The learning is on but for sure at the independence of the learner. Likewise, preparation members and workshop crowds have been getting some information for quite a long time. So I chose to gather the ten best apparatuses and standards I know into a short, sharp course. The most significant way to deal with flourishing in a VUCA world is the Pareto Principle, the 80:20 standard. The 80:20 principle says that you get 80% of the worth from the best 20% of the thoughts, and we end up applying it at the point when you use it well. In this way, here is the best 20%. Apply it well, and you'll significantly affect your work prosperity. Learning how to learn is the new priority.

The Uncertain Times!

How? What? When?

"There are two things we can say with conviction about the future: it will be extraordinary. Like never before, pioneers need to explore new testing times, a reviving speed of progress, expanding assumptions, and a rising tide of quickly developing conditions. This unique and distinctive climate (VUCA) is moving pioneers to discover better approaches to lead their associations and make supported progress. Because of these conditions, there is a hunger for administration. Yet, pioneers face a tornado climate loaded with incredible freedoms and overwhelming difficulties to lead their kin and associations.

If I share the quote by Prof Sattar Bawany (2019), the Fourth Industrial Revolution (Industry 4.0) addresses a blend of Artificial Intelligence, Robotics, Cyber-Physical Systems and the Internet-of-Things (IoT). Authority 4.0 is about pioneers making their advanced change procedure and guaranteeing it is lined up with their business and development plans. This is accomplished by successfully showing the set-up of next-generation initiative capabilities that incorporate basic reasoning, imaginative speculation, and enthusiastic and social knowledge abilities like sympathy and relationship with the board.

They were driving in the Fourth Industrial Revolution (Industry 4.0) spin around overseeing difficulties in a business climate that is profoundly problematic, progressively computerised and overwhelmingly unstable, unsure, mind-boggling and vague (VUCA). Innovative headways in artificial brainpower, mechanical technology, sharing stages and the Internet of Things adjust plans of action and businesses. These progressions are occurring at an uncommon speed. Pioneers at all levels need to foster the significant capabilities and abilities to effectively adjust to new fundamental factors when driving in a troublesome VUCA World.

VUCA is an abbreviation that arose out of the military during the 1990s. It portrays the "haze of war" — the turbulent conditions experienced in an advanced combat zone. Its importance to pioneers in business is evident, as these conditions elucidate the climate where the company is led each day. Authority, not surprisingly, including making a dream, isn't sufficient in a VUCA world. TEACHING IN THE VUCA WORLD, a card priority fetches the world of uncertainties. The new world order of VOLATILE, UNCERTAIN, COMPLEX, AMBIGUOUS approaches reflect new everyday learning and exploring the novel order of working.

- *Volatile:*

Things change eccentrically, out of nowhere, particularly for the more regrettable.

- *Uncertain:*

Critical data isn't known or clear; suspicious, hazy about the current circumstance and future results; not ready to be depended upon.

- *Complex:*

Many unique and associated parts: different key choice factors, the connection between assorted specialists, development, variation, coevolution, feeble signs.

- *Ambiguous:*

Open to more than one translation, the significance of an occasion can be perceived unexpectedly.

Driving in a VUCA world not just gives a moving climate to pioneers to work and for chief advancement program to have an effect: it likewise gives an essential scope of new abilities. The new truth brings about the acknowledgement that new and various skills are required for pioneers to prevail in this new typical. As educators, we need to guide our students and parents towards new destinations, which may include:

Flourish amid unpredictability, vulnerability, intricacy and equivocalness.

Recognise the need to choose what you centre around

Construct an essential organisation of essential contacts

Realise were to work at your pinnacle

Output your frame of reference for changes, patterns, dangers and openings

Bridle the basic achievement framework for life during the transition; the Powerhouse Loop

The Online Teaching and Learning with the Parents Support

Well, finally to explore the wonders amongst the PANDEMIC and the readiness to the VUCA world, without a doubt, the word VUCA causes some cocked eyebrows and characterizes the prepared idea of shock, an evoke stun, shock, or offense, ordinarily through whimsical activities or words. The expression regularly recommends negative consideration or judgment, however my dear companions, serves a reality today. As a head of a school, I discover checking and testing easily of solace for the educators to be locked in and module to the learning situation. The range deceives our arrangement which screens thus, training has changed drastically, with the unmistakable ascent of e-learning, whereby educating is attempted distantly and on advanced stages. The paging is organized and characterized with the characteristic of conveying the classes without any difficulty and solace of their takers.

The target of this module enacts learning concerning the Leading Change in a Pandemic VUCA World specifically. The common vision and the methodology characterizes the destinations with introduction of understanding the idea in Visualizing the learning incredibly. It incorporates about the model to deal with the world through VOCA in the COVID period. Step by step instructions to prepare pioneers to oversee through. The idea represents the Volatility, Uncertainty, Complexity, Ambiguity, as VOCA practically speaking.

Without a doubt as training suppliers, our great work is to help everybody in giving quality schooling to all even in these extraordinary occasions. The reality lies that educators will in general do twofold and surprisingly threefold the task to convey. As we as a whole scramble to adapt to the quickly evolving COVID-19 circumstance, a significant number of us are unexpectedly taking on jobs as all day guardians and substitute educators likewise

with the walk for the rush to convey.

The live streaming which the guardians requested sometime in the distant past mirror the ascent of new requests and wants. What is required is the need towards conveying the exercises to give every understudy customized criticism and work on, setting them up to benefit from study hall guidance.

Happy Learning to all on priority.

Ref:

https://www.asmaindia.in/slc-2021/speaker/dr-dheeraj-mehrotra/

CHAPTER FOUR

The New Age Learning Spectrum

At the rate at which technology is progressing, Students entering school today will find themselves two decades from now in occupations that do not exist today. We had never imagined Flipkart, Amazon, Uber, swiggy, or even Google or Facebook two decades back.

Coding today is catching fire! Anyone nowadays can learn to code and create their website or even their own business in the future. Educational institutions must focus on their day-to-day operations and shape their vision on how they will better use technology for enhancing the learning process. Today's students have an entirely different world view to previous generations, having grown up in a world full of choice and limitless options. They have high expectations, demanding fast, easy access to content wherever they are.

Gamification has added a more creative, dynamic and innovative element to learning. These activities can potentially turn an otherwise routine teaching-learning process into an imaginative exercise that will motivate students to work harder and provide teachers with valuable insight into student performance. Video-sharing websites, such as YouTube, also offer educational videos that students rely on for doubt solving and learning.

Today's students need more profound cognitive skills in priority areas such as creativity and problem solving and social-emotional skills such as relationship building, self-awareness, and self-recognition since they support academic learning and promote well-being. Technology can play an increasingly critical role in students learning and how educators support them to meet these needs.

In a country like India with such a vast population, even if teachers and schools believe in the power of personalised learning and are motivated to individualise instruction, it is not always clear how to do so for hundreds or thousands of students. One-on-one mentoring is a highly effective way to personalise learning, for instance. Still, it is not feasible for working with large student populations when the focus is more on time-bound syllabus completion and assessments. Instead, schools can rely on technology-enabled systems and

student-driven, which is a compelling way to provide personalised learning on a large scale.

CHAPTER FIVE

Harnessing Creativity Within Classrooms

To Teach is to preach. The subjective modulation task the learning regime to years and years of research with leverage of connecting within the learners. Teach children to teach themselves, and foster a love for learning. So, why are there so many students who cave in and quit? Why are the student dropout rates at an astonishingly high rate? Whatever happened to parental involvement and budgets that generally supported a solid, quality education?

To the pride of learning, I ask, what are students expected to learn from their classroom experiences? What do they genuinely need to know to be successful and prepared for college or career readiness? Current research shows that Deep Learning and Close Reading techniques significantly improve academic results for all students involved. How do we, as educators, foster these and other researched-based programs in more schools?

Quality instruction is a vital component of quality education; however, not all learning is acquired and grasped inside the classroom environment. Indeed, teachers should encourage students to explore, be critical thinkers, and become learner-centred. An exceptional teacher focuses on classroom teaching, community building, and individualised mentorship.

The time says it all; the page is sure with the inception of technology in education. However, irrespective of the perseverance, determination, and patient use of highly qualified educators, ultimately, students will get out of their education what they put in. The philosophical dilemma doesn't exist with the concept of inspiring the already gifted student or illuminating the students who have a passion for learning. The true challenge of teaching is engaging and nurturing the love of learning for all students, especially those who have academically and emotionally "checked out."

The solace remains towards bringing learning within the four walls of the classrooms from the BLACK SCREENS of the kids, desktops, laptops, and now the palmtops via mobile. Students need to attain more than rigorous content objectives. There needs to be a paradigm shift towards less palpable skills and a greater emphasis on creative thinking, collaboration, and problem-solving coupled with thorough teaching and instruction. Students will primarily benefit when they reflect upon and evaluate ways to improve their overall comprehension. Teachers should also seek beneath and beyond the expectations of standards to teach the whole child.

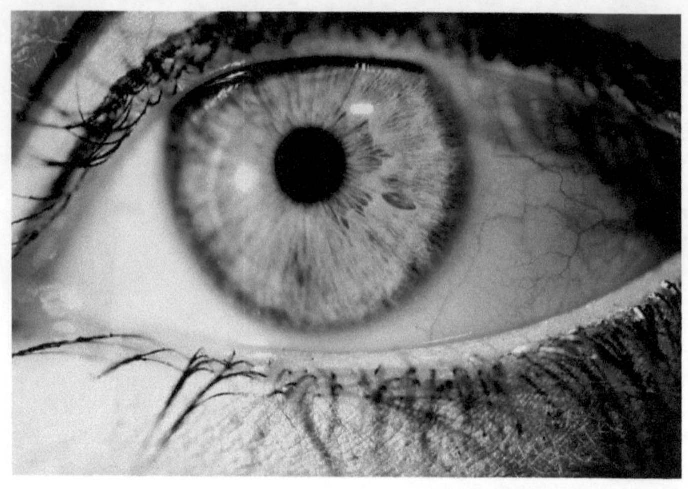

As a lifelong learner, I delight in being the student and the teacher. I embrace the challenges of pedagogy and an academic arena of active learning and teamwork. The framework needs real-world experiences, discussions, analysis, and evaluations within quality instruction and education.

Far to believe but for sure, Engaging students to be equipped to grasp the material, embrace technology and facilitate classroom dialogue strategically is the pinnacle. The crux of my educational and professional endeavours has fashioned my teaching perspective, and ultimately, students should be at the core of all teaching philosophies. Creativity within classrooms is activated with the perception of engagement with all the kids and not just with the few bright minds. The initiative has to be to catch them young and innocent. It is high time that we approach the mechanism to Teach One-Teach All as a prime scope towards gaining connection with the kids in the classrooms.

We, the teachers/ educators, start reflecting on our pedagogies concerning the new age demands and policies. The children engage and tend to RUN away from Teachers they don't like. They only like the subject if they want

the teachers. Hence, it is requisite for all the teachers to bring in a ***WOW*** *capsule expose' within and outside the classrooms incorporated through creativity and spectrum of learning to learn as a hobby rather than an occasional occurrence.*

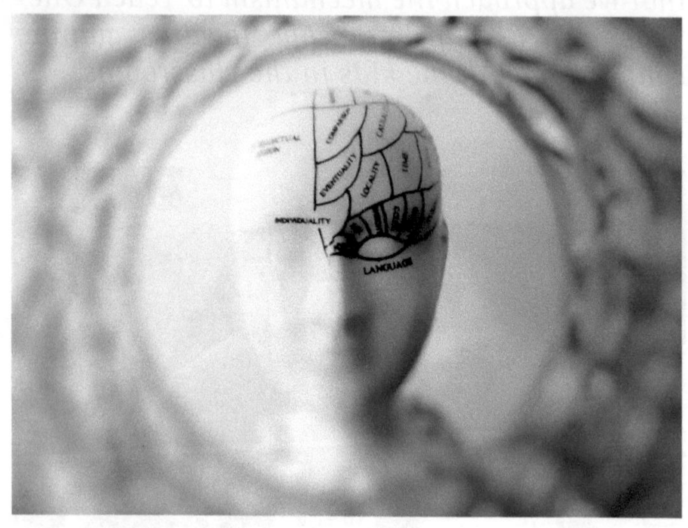

Let learning be creative, experiential above all, and fertile. To teach in this VUCA world is greater a challenge for the majority today with the march of expectation from the stakeholders. The task is to reflect on how to make the best in use and the delivery to make it functional for the learners to be engaged and communicative.

CHAPTER SIX

The Brave New World

With the greatest of pleasure, the learning has become more so independent with the fast pace to furnish the academic demands on priority. Tech dependence is a priority. One has to have a stellar resume and looks to grow with the march of time.

The brave new world of the new normal has defined learning as a spectrum over a couple of years post-pandemic. One has to exemplify the everyday culture with the significant dependence on technology.

What comes to my mind in this VUCA world is the importance of the poem by Rudyard Kipling, IF.

IF,

BY RUDYARD KIPLING

('Brother Square-Toes'—Rewards and Fairies)

If you can keep your head when all about you

Are you losing theirs and blaming it on you,

If you can trust yourself when all men doubt you,

But make allowance for their doubting too;

If you can wait and not be tired by waiting,

Or being lied about, don't deal in lies,

Or being hated, don't give way to hating,

And yet don't look too good, nor talk too wise:

If you can dream—and not make dreams your master;

If you can think—and not make thoughts your aim;

If you can meet with Triumph and Disaster

And treat those two impostors just the same;

If you can bear to hear the truth you've spoken

Twisted by knaves to make a trap for fools,

Or watch the things you gave your life to, broken,

And stoop and build them up with worn-out tools:

If you can make one heap of all your winnings

And risk it on one turn of pitch-and-toss,

And lose, and start again at your beginnings

And never breathe a word about your loss;

If you can force your heart and nerve and sinew

To serve your turn long after they are gone,

And so hold on when there is nothing in you

Except for the Will, which says to them: 'Hold on!'

If you can talk with crowds and keep your virtue,

Or walk with Kings—nor lose the common touch,

If neither foes nor loving friends can hurt you,

If all men count with you, but none too much;

If you can fill the unforgiving minute

With sixty seconds' worth of distance run,

Yours is the Earth and everything that's in it,

And—which is more—you'll be a Man, my son!

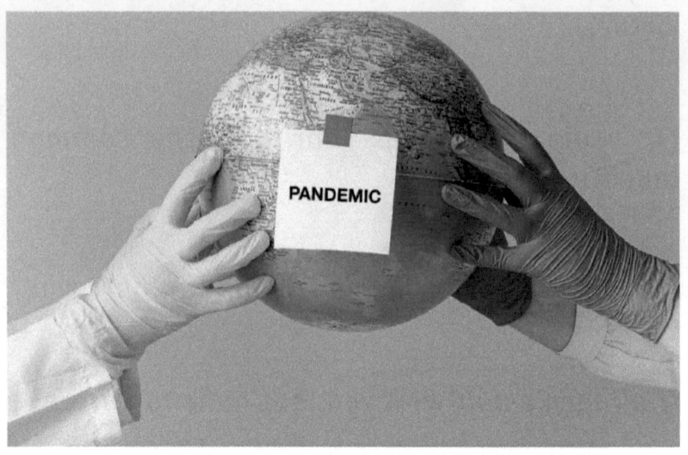

At the rate at which technology is progressing, Students entering school today will find themselves two decades from now in occupations that do not exist today. We had never imagined Flipkart, Amazon, Uber, swiggy, or even Google or Facebook two decades back. Coding today is catching fire! Anyone nowadays can learn to code and create their website or even their own business in the future. Educational institutions must focus on their day-to-day operations and shape their vision on how they will better use technology for enhancing the learning process. Today's students have an entirely different world view to previous generations, having grown up in a world full of choice and limitless options. They have high expectations, demanding fast, easy

access to content wherever they are.

Gamification has added a more creative, dynamic and innovative element to learning. These activities can potentially turn an otherwise routine teaching-learning process into an imaginative exercise that will motivate students to work harder and provide teachers with valuable insight into student performance. Video-sharing websites, such as YouTube, also offer an array of educational videos which students rely on for doubt solving and learning.

Today's students need more profound cognitive skills in priority areas such as creativity and problem solving and social-emotional skills such as relationship building, self-awareness, and self-recognition since they support academic learning and promote well-being. Technology can play an increasingly critical role in students learning and how educators support them to meet these needs. In a country like India with such a vast population, even if teachers and schools believe in the power of personalised learning and are motivated to individualise instruction, it is not always clear how to do so for hundreds or thousands of students. One-on-one mentoring is a highly effective way to personalise learning, for

instance. Still, it is not feasible for working with large student populations when the focus is more on time-bound syllabus completion and assessments. Instead, schools can rely on technology-enabled systems and student-driven, which is a compelling way to provide personalised learning on a large scale. The preparedness to face the uncertain has to be a priority now both from the students and the teachers point of view in particular.

CHAPTER SEVEN

Achieving a Student-Driven Classroom

Friends, the learning has taken its pace to the majority who, by chance or tribes, get governed by the Google Generation of today. Alas, to the say, the teachers are no longer the fountain of knowledge but an artistic adults to manage the classroom discipline.

The teachers who motivate, differentiate, make content relevant and leave no student behind are more important than any other factor. Students like the subject only when they like the teacher, hence a directly proportional element within a classroom. The drive by the teacher in the class with the vocabulary is signified by the equilibrium of learning together rather than teaching. They say, "Teachers know the best", activates wisdom just in the say but in action. The sole reason for this far-fetched approach lies in the nutshell element of a straightforward process of open knowledge, which is unrestricted, versatile and dual with surprises. The satisfaction and the wow part within classrooms only prevails where there is a taste

of "It is in the book, Ma'am, tell us something new!" As a teacher, it is our wisdom to teach the "I can do approach" instead of the "I shall try approach", which is universally possible only when we use kind words in the class. Compliment each kid, especially the difficult ones. That might be the only positive thing they hear all day.

Activating a student-oriented rather than a task-oriented classroom requires more of a connection, a relationship with the student. At times apologising to students is a learning moment. If we want kids with character, we must model it to them with others, as character counts. The experiences shared in totality that

a genuine apology requires freely admitting fault, fully accepting responsibility, a humbled asking for forgiveness, immediately changing the behaviour, and actively rebuilding the trust. The dose of willingness to explore knowledge is what is desired rather than sharing contents from the book.

When students appear crusaders of expertise, the teachers need to act like a facilitator more but strict disciplinarian in particular. It must be made clear to everyone that there is no expiry date for hunger for learning. Let yearning for knowledge be a priority rather than an occasional occurrence. Also, the teachers must explore the power of curing

ignorance as to the chief element of choice in every interaction with the students, teachers, peers and parents. It is never too late to make yourself better; it should be the priority. The segment of reality lies in engaging the children in the class with no fear but intimacy and a feeling of pride both by the students and the teachers. To the real concerns, fear kills dreams more than failure ever will, which should be mounted on priority by the masses. The children should be made to enjoy the classroom session with engagement and knowledge sharing using ICT tools and techniques of the cyber world and making their Online reputation management a reality.

Today's students are no longer kids but young adults and hence need recognition as individuals and partners in the learning process. Critical thinking must be one of the prime qualities of the children as it is among the first causes for change, but is a parish in schools- for no other reason than it conditions the mind to suspect the form and function of everything it sees, including the classroom scenario, all what is taught and discussed. As a teacher, it is our prime requisites to make progress visible, adjust grading practices, model desired habits and don't get carried away with the politics of the school, the students and the parents. Hey, the voice violates, the Principal's lobby is rushed for, is there any debating subject rises or fumes up. The school principal is targeted and reassured support to the students, as ever be.

BACK TO
SCHOOL

To govern and sense student's friendly classroom, the teachers need to check on their share of the day, of some new vocabulary and make a haze to the fact that the students should be held accountable for the number and the quality of questions students ask and pursue during the teaching-learning process. From Good Morning Wishing to the, Thank you, children, the time and share has to be so friendly and empowering to make them take home moments of joy and some attributes to share with their parents. This must be a priority. Teachers need to showcase in action that they are not perfect and never will be. They must take risks with their teaching, and failing must be a part of the learning process. We face the Google Generation, which empowers self and is not dependent on either the library or the teacher; fortunately, I doubt my words too.

The beautiful words help our children use a wide range of captivating words in their writings. We must not blame them for their handwriting and knowledge limitations. Instead, they must be part and parcel of their learning. Also, to create a rapport with the students, the teaching tools in practice by the teachers need to be evaluated concerning whether the usage during the lesson is appropriate. With this, the teacher's subject knowledge, enthusiasm, questioning methods, exposition, and problem-solving related to the multilevel dimension for judging. The teachers as facilitators explore and expose the learning objectives in a big bang way via repartees and the responses generated after every class or via

the Parents' Teachers' Meetings on jolt and achievements. Let us conclude the fact that children will love and explore their presence in the classrooms only when given the recognition of individual concerns; teachers must call the kids by their first names keeping them at pace to importance rather than experiencing the only preface with them at the time of the roll calls and that too with referencing through roll numbers.

The choice is ours, engage or enrage! Let quality be the taste forever instead of being just an occasional occurrence. The priority must be to create a WOW classroom with the tongue of "You can do wonders", "You can do it!" and above all ", All my students are the best of the students, and I am proud of them".

Happy Teaching! In the new normal Post COVID!!

About The Authors

Dheeraj Mehrotra has been honoured with the President of India's National Teacher Award in the year 2006 and the Best Science Teacher State Award, Innovation in Education for his inception of Six Sigma In Education by Education Watch, New Delhi and Education World- Best Teacher Award, BOLT Learner Teacher Award by Air India, 'Innovation in Education Award 2016' among others. He has developed over 150 FREE EDUCATIONAL MOBILE Apps for the Google Play Store exclusively for academics. This work has been recognised by the LIMCA BOOK OF RECORDS & INDIA BOOK OF RECORDS. Dr Mehrotra is presently working as a PRINCIPAL at KUNWARS GLOBAL SCHOOL, Lucknow, in India. He is an active TEDx speaker. As a premium UDEMY Instructor, he has also developed over 450 courses and is catering to over 8 Lakh students from 180 plus countries. He can be visited at www.authordheerajmehrotra.com.

Dr Ushavati Shetty- A mother, A seasoned, goal-driven, versatile, motivated, dedicated and dynamic visionary Educator with more than two decades of experience working in reputed CBSE, ICSE, STATE BOARD Institutions with International Exposure as well. Dr Shetty, a self-directed, action-oriented, enthusiastic learner, has expertise in Psychology. She is an Eloquent Bonafide speaker, blogger, and trainer and has conducted various sessions for students and teachers. She has been honoured & Felicitated at multiple prestigious forums. She is frequently invited as a Guest speaker at various Prominent Educational Conferences and international platforms. She is a recipient of a few prestigious awards. A notable writer and has articles published in multiple well-known magazines and leading newspapers—currently the Principal for Navodaya English High School & Jr. College, Maharashtra.

Books By The Same Author

www.authordheerajmehrotra.com

9 798886 670370

Printed by Libri Plureos GmbH in Hamburg, Germany